no matter what

Music by Andrew Lloyd Webber. Lyrics by Jim Steinman.

Unhurried

A A7 D

Bm A

A Bm/A

No mat-ter what they tell us, no mat-ter what they do,
If on-ly tears were laugh-ter, if on-ly night was day,

Bm D/E E Esus4 E A

no mat-ter what they teach us, what we be-lieve is true.
if on-ly prayers were an-swered then we would hear God say.

A
No mat - ter what they call us, how - ev - er they at -
No mat - ter what they tell you, no mat - ter what they
Bm/A
Bm
D/E
E
- tack, no mat - ter where they take us,
do, no mat - ter what they teach you,
Esus4
E
A
we'll find our own way back. I can't de - ny what I
what you be - lieve is true. And I will keep you safe
A7
D
be - lieve, I can't be what I'm not.
and strong and shel - tered from the storm.

a different beat 8
all that i need 13
ben 24
coming home now 18
father and son 27
i love the way you love me 32
key to my life 37
love me for a reason 42
no matter what 3
picture of you 47
so good 60
when all is said and done 52
words 56

boyzone greatest hits so far...

Wise Publications
London / New York / Sydney / Paris / Copenhagen / Madrid

Exclusive Distributors:

Music Sales Limited
8/9 Frith Street,
London W1V 5TZ, England.

Music Sales Pty Limited
120 Rothschild Avenue
Rosebery, NSW 2018, Australia.

Order No. AM949300
ISBN 0-7119-7354-7

Book design by Michael Bell Design.

Printed in Great Britain by
Printwise (Haverhill) Limited, Suffolk.

Bm
D/E
E
Esus4
E7
I know our love's for - ev - er,
I know no mat - ter what.
No mat - ter where it's bar - ren
our dream is be - ing born.
1.
2.
A
A
C
f Instrumental
Dm
Dm/G
G7
G
C
F/C

C
F/C
C
Dm
No mat-ter who they fol - low,
no mat-ter where they lead,
F/G
G7
Gsus4
G7
no mat-ter how they judge us
I'll be eve - ry one you need.
C
C7/E
No mat - ter if the sun don't shine,
F
C/E
Dm
or if the skies are blue.
No mat - ter what the

F/G G7 Gsus4 G7 C
ending, my life be - gan with you. I
C C7/E F rall. C/E
can't de - ny what I be - lieve, I can't be what I'm not.
Colla voce
Dm G7
I know this love's for ev - er, That's all that mat - ters now no mat - ter
a tempo
C2
Repeat to fade
No no mat - ter no. No no mat - ter no.
what. No no mat- - ter what. No no mat-

a different beat

Words & Music by Martin Brannigan, Stephen Gately, Ronan Keating, Shane Lynch, Keith Duffy & Ray Hedges.

♩= 88
D♭
fr4
Let's not for - get this place,
let's not ne -

G♭
D♭
fr4
glect our race,
let u - ni - ty be - come,

A♭sus4
fr4
A♭
fr4
life on earth be one.
1. So let me

D♭
fr4
D♭sus4
D♭
G♭
take your hand,
(Verse 2 see block lyric)
we are but grains of sand,
born through the
Absus4
A♭
winds of time,
giv-en a spe-cial sign.
So
let's take a stand and look a-round us now,
peo-ple.
So
let's take a stand and look a-round us now,
peo-ple.
Ee-

D♭
fr4
G♭
B♭m7
yea oh, ee - yea oh, ee - yea oh, by - yah.
A♭
fr4
D♭
fr4
G♭
Ee - yea oh, ee - yea oh, ee -
(To a dif - fer - ent beat.)
B♭m7
1.
A♭
fr4
2.
A♭
fr4
yea oh, by - yah. 2. Hu-man - i -
D♭/F
G♭
A♭
fr4
B♭m
D♭/F
G♭
I've seen the rain fall in Af - ri - ca, I've touched the snows of A -

A♭
fr4
D♭
fr4
D♭/F
G♭
las - - - ka,
I've felt the mists of Ni -
B♭m
C♭add9
fr6
a - ga - ra,
now I be - lieve
in you.
Ee -
3
(2º) How far we've come
yea oh, ee - yea oh, ee -
B♭m7
and how far to go.
yea oh, by - yah.
Ee -

Verse 2:
Humanity has lost face,
Let's understand its grace,
Each day, one at a time,
Each life, including mine.

Let's take a stand and look around us now,
People,
So let's take a stand and look around us now,
People, oh people, oh people.

all that i need

Words & Music by Evan Rogers & Carl Sturken.

G
Am
like a song out of time, and there you are stand-
Dm7
G11
C
G
-ing in front of my eyes. How could I be such a fool to
Am
Dm7
G11
C
let go of love and break all of the rules? Girl, when you walked
G
Am
Dm7
G11
out that door, left a hole in my heart and now I know for sure;

C
G
You're the air that I breathe girl, you're all that I need.
Am
Dm7
G11
C
And I wan-na thank you la - dy.
You're the words that I read,
G
Am
Dm7
G11
you're the light that I see,
and your love is all that I need.
Am
Fmaj7
B♭maj7

Dm7
G11
C
G
You're the air that I breath girl you're all that I need.
Am
Dm7
G11
And I wan - na thank you la - dy.
C
G
You're the words that I read, you're the light that I see,
Am
Dm7
G11
and your love is all that I need.

Verse 2:
I was searching in vain, playing your game
Had no-one else but myself left to blame
You came into my world, no diamonds or pearls
Could ever replace what you gave to me girl
Just like a castle of sand
Girl I almost let love
Slip right out of my hand
And just like a flower needs rain
I will stand by your side
Through the joy and the pain.

You're the air that I breathe *etc.*

coming home now

Words & Music by Stephen Gately, Ronan Keating, Michael Graham, Shane Lynch & Keith Duffy.

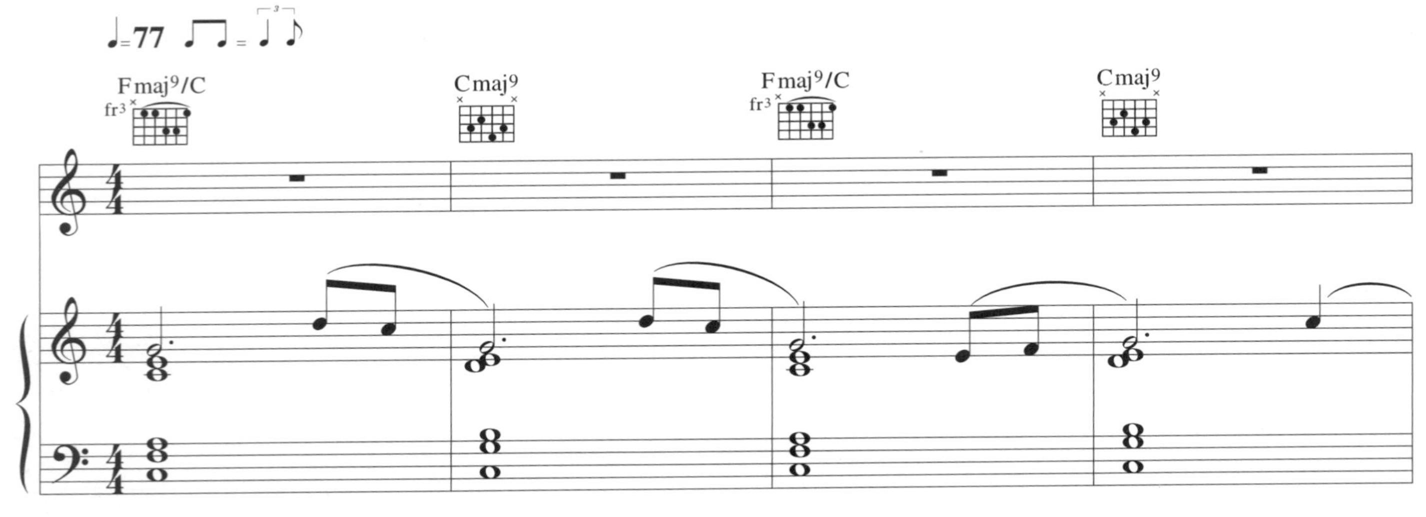

♩=77
Fmaj9/C
fr3
Cmaj9
Fmaj9/C
fr3
Cmaj9

Fmaj9/C
fr3
Cmaj9
Fmaj9/C
fr3
Weeks, days, hours, min- utes till I'll be home. Weeks, days,

Cmaj9
Fmaj9/C
fr3
Cmaj9
hours, min- utes till I'll be home. Da da da da da da.
Da da da da da da.

Fmaj9/C
Cmaj9
Fmaj9/C
Da da da da da da. Da da da da da da. A kiss on the cheek in the old town park,
Cmaj9
Fmaj9/C
carved your name in the shape of a heart, walked to-ge-ther hand in hand,
Cmaj9
Fmaj9/C
Cmaj9
I did-n't feel the rain. And there's a
Fmaj9
Cmaj7/E
Fmaj9
pic-ture, girl, that hangs in-side my mind, and there's a let-ter, girl, say I'm do-ing

C/E
G/E
Fmaj9
fr2
Cmaj7/E
fine. And there's a pic - ture, girl, that hangs in - side my mind, and there's a
Fmaj9
fr2
Gsus4
G
let - ter, girl, say I'm do - ing fine. And I'm com - ing home
Fmaj9
fr2
Cmaj7/E
now, it's been so long now. Gon - na get there some -
Fmaj9
fr2
C/E
To Coda
- how, pray - ing you'll be there. Com - ing home

Fmaj9
fr2
Cmaj7/E
now, it's been so long now. Gon-na get there some-
Fmaj9
fr2
C/E
G
how, pray-ing you'll be there. Weeks, days till I'll be there.
Fmaj9/C
fr3
Cmaj9
Child-ren on the streets still play-ing their games, the smiles on their fa-ces have ne-ver changed.
Fmaj9/C
fr3
Cmaj9
I hope it's all the same,

Fmaj9/C
fr3
Cmaj9
D.%. al Coda
I did - n't leave in vain.
And there's a
Coda
Fmaj9
fr2
Cmaj7/E
now,
it's been so long
now.
Gon - na get there some -
Fmaj9
fr2
C/E
- how,
and this is where I'll
stay,
and this is where I'll
Fmaj9
fr2
Cmaj9/E
Fmaj9
fr2
stay.
I'm
Spoken:
"Dearly close words: I really want to see you. You're in my heart when overseas.
I feel you close, and not so far. Soon we'll be together, and this time it's forever.

G
Fmaj9
fr2
C
on my way, and I'm com-ing home now, been so long now. Gon-na get there some-
Fmaj9
fr2
C
- how, pray-ing you'll be there. Com-ing home
Fmaj9
fr2
Cmaj7/E
now, it's been so long now. Gon-na get there some-
Fmaj9
fr2
2º To Fade
C/E
- how, and this is where I'll stay. And I'll be com-ing home

ben

Words by Don Black. Music by Walter Scharf.

♩=74

Db Gb Db Gb Db Gb Db Gb

Db Ab/C Db

1. Ben, the two of us need look no more, we both found what we were
(Verses 2 & 3 see block lyric)

Ab/C Db Cm7add4 F/A

look-ing for. With a friend to call my own, I'll nev-er be a-

C♭(♭5)
B♭7
A7(♭5)
A♭7
D♭
G♭/D♭
3º To Coda ⊕
lone and you my friend will see you got a friend in me.
(3º) A
(You got a friend in
1.
2.
D♭
G♭/D♭
E♭m7add4
A♭/C
me.)
me.)
I used to say
D♭maj7
E♭m7add4
A♭/C
D♭
"I" and "me".
Now it's "us",
now it's "we".
E♭m7add4
A♭/C
D♭maj7
E♭m7add4
A♭/C
D♭
D.%. al Coda

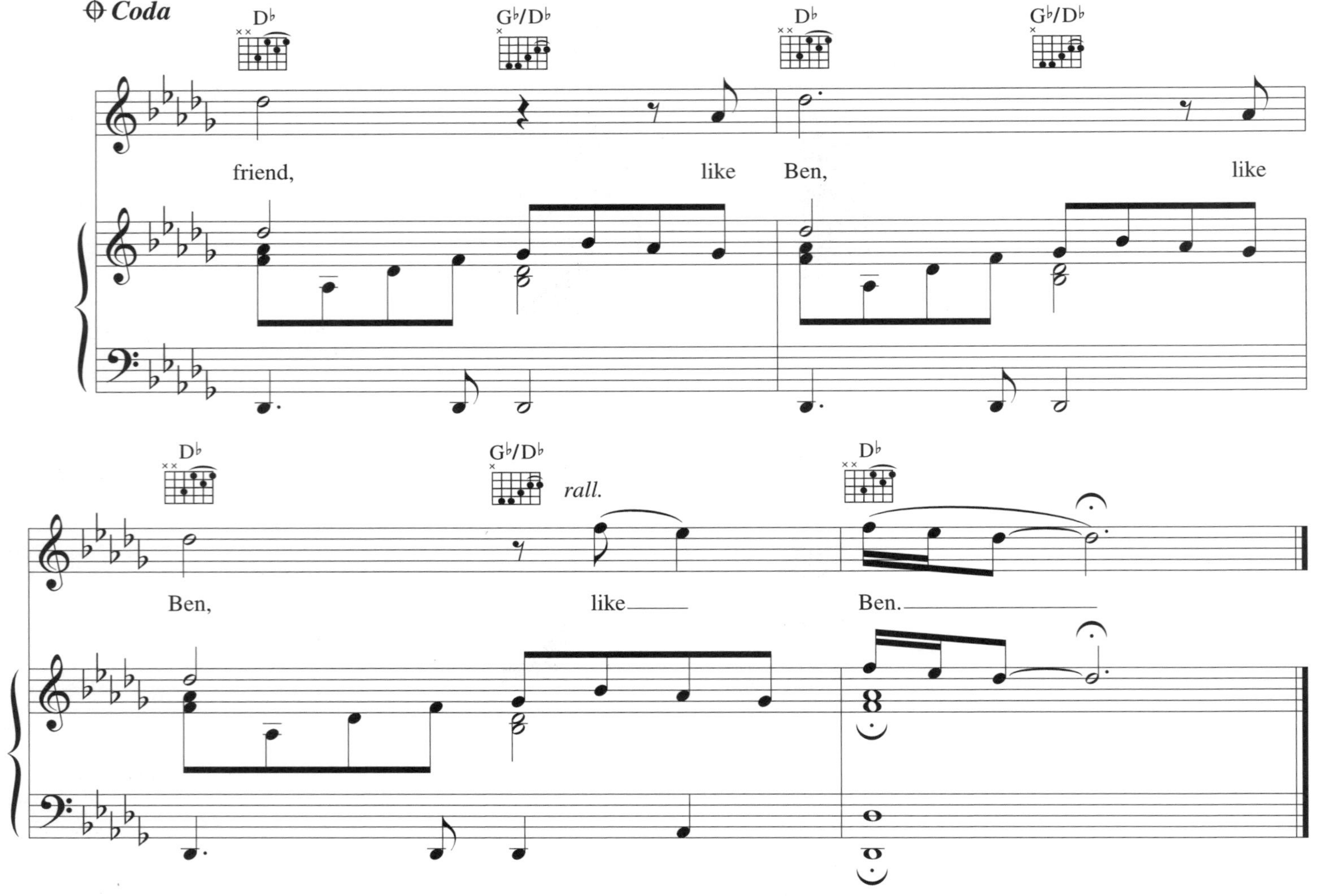

Verse 2:
Ben, you're always running here and there,
You feel you're not wanted anywhere.
If you ever look behind
And don't like what you find,
There's one thing you should know:
You've got a place to go.

Verse 3:
Ben, most people would turn you away,
I don't listen to a word they say.
They don't see you as I do,
I wish they would try to;
I'm sure they'd think again
If they had a friend like Ben.

father and son

Words & Music by Cat Stevens.

♩=72
1. It's not
E♭
fr3
B♭
A♭
fr4
Fm7
time to make a change; just re - lax, take it ea - sy. You're still
(Verse 2 see block lyric)
E♭
fr3
Cm7
fr3
Fm7
B♭
young, that's your fault; there's so much you have to know. Find a girl,

E♭
B♭
A♭
Fm7
set - tle down; if you want, you can mar - ry. Look at me:
1.
E♭
Cm7
Fm7
B♭
I am old but I'm hap - py. 2. I was
2.
E♭
Cm
B♭
E♭
A♭
be here to - mor - row, but your dreams may not.
E♭
A♭
E♭
Gm7
How can I try to ex - plain? When I do
(Verse 4 see block lyric)

A♭
fr4
Fm7
E♭
fr3
Cm7
fr3
he turns a-way a-gain. Well, it's al - ways been the same, same old
Fm7
B♭
E♭
fr3
Gm7
fr3
sto - ry. From the mo - ment I could talk, I was or -
A♭
fr4
Fm7
E♭
fr3
Cm7
fr3
To Coda
- dered to lis - ten; now there's a way, and I know that I
B♭
E♭
fr3
B♭
A♭
fr4
have to go a - way. I know I have to

E♭
A♭
E♭
A♭
fr3
fr4
go.
3. It's not
B♭
Fm7
time to make a change, just sit down and take it slow - ly. You're still
Cm7
young, that's your fault; there's so much you have to go through. Find a girl,
set - tle down; if you want, you can mar - ry. Look at me

Eb
Cm7
Fm7
Bb
D.%. al Coda
I am old but I'm hap - py.
4. All the
Coda
Bb
Eb
Bb
Ab
Eb
have to go a - way.
I know I have to go.

Verse 2:
I was once like you are now;
And I know that it's not easy
To be calm when you've found something going on.
But take your time, think a lot;
Think of everything you've got.
For you will still be here tomorrow,
But your dreams may not.

Verse 4:
All the times that I've cried,
Keeping all the things I knew inside;
And it's hard, but it's harder to ignore it.
If they were right I'd agree,
But it's them they know, not me;
Now there's a way, and I know
That I have to go away.
I know I have to go.

i love the way you love me

Words & Music by Chuck Cannon & Victoria Shaw.

♩= 84
A
F♯m7
Dmaj7
C♯m7
fr4
Bm7
F♯m7
G/F
Fmaj7
E11
E
E11
E7
Aadd9
F♯m7add11
1. I like the feel of your name on my lips and I like the sound of your sweet

Dadd9
fr2
gen - tle kiss, the way that your fin - gers run through my hair and
E11
E
Dadd9/F♯
fr2
E7/G♯
how your scent lin - gers ev - en when you're not there. 2. And
Aadd9
F♯m7add11
I like the way your eyes dance when you laugh and how you'll en - joy your two
(Verse 3 see block lyrics)
Dadd9
fr2
hour bath and how you con - vinced me to dance in the rain with

E11
E
E11
E
ev - 'ry - one watch - in' like we were in - sane. But I
Dmaj9
fr4
E7
A
love the way you love me
oh ba - by.
Dmaj9
fr4
Strong and wild,
E7
A
slow and ea - sy,
heart and soul,

D
E11
To Coda
so com - plete - ly. I love the way you love
1.
A
Dm/F
E7
2.
A
me, yeah. me.
E/G♯
fr2
D
E
(So listen to me now) And I could list a mil - lion things
A
D
I'd love to like a - bout you. (A - bout you) But they all come down to

A/C♯
Bm7
E11
E7
D.%. al Coda
one rea - son, I could ne - ver live with - out you. I
Coda
A
E/G♯
Gsus2
D/F♯
me.
I
Dadd9
Free time
E11
Aadd9
love the way that you love me.

Verse 3:
And I like the sound of old R and B
You roll your eyes when I'm slightly off key
And I like the innocent way that you cry
From sappy old movies you've seen thousands of times.

But I love *etc.*

key to my life

Words & Music by Martin Brannigan, Stephen Gately, Ronan Keating, Michael Graham & Ray Hedges.

Aadd9
Bm7/E
won't let you go a - way.
Aadd9
F♯m add4
Stain on the desk - top where the cof-fee cup lay, and mem-'ries of you for -
(Verse 2 see block lyric)
Bm7
ev - er will stay. And the scent of your per - fume and the smile on your face will re - main.
Aadd9
Dadd9
fr2
And I ne - ver gave up hope when

E
Dadd9
fr2
things got me down but I just bit on my lip as my
E
A
Dadd9
fr2
face be-gan to frown 'cause that was just my pride and I've
E
Bm7add4
E
no-thing left to hide and now that way is clear and all I want to say, is.
A
D
E
A
F♯m
Bm7
All of my life the doors have been closed now and all of my dreams have been

E
A
D
locked up in - side, but you came a - long and cap- tured my heart girl,
To Coda
1.
E
Gadd9
Dadd9/F♯
Aadd9
you're the key to my life.
2.
life.
Girl you know that I feel for you, there ain't no - thing that I would - n't do,
Gadd9
stop the thun - der and the pour - ing rain, you're the one that's gon - na stop the pain.
Asus4

Verse 2:
Year after year was blaming myself
For what I'd done just thought of myself
I know that you'll understand this was all my fault
Don't go away.

love me for a reason

Words & Music by John Bristol, Wade Brown Jr & David Jones Jr.

♩= 78
A
E/G♯
fr2
Em/G
D/F♯
A/E
D
A/E
Esus4
E
A
E/G♯
1. Girl, when you hold me,
(Verses 2 & 3 see block lyric)
Em/G
D/F♯
A/E
D
A/C♯
Bm7
E
how you con-trol me; you bend and you fold me an-y way you please.

A
E/G♯
Em/G
D/F♯
It must be ea - sy for you, the love-ly things that you do are
A/E
D
A/E
Esus4
E
just a pas - time for you, I could ne - ver be.
C♯m7
F♯m7
Bm7
D
E
And I ne - ver know, girl, if I should stay or go, 'cos the games
C♯m7
F♯m7
Bm7
A/C♯
D
D/E
that you play keep driv - ing me a - way.

A
C♯m7
fr4
D
A
Don't love me for fun, girl, let me be the one, girl,
Bm7
A/C♯
D
Esus4
E
To Coda
love me for a rea - son, let the rea - son be love.
A
C♯m7
fr4
D
A
Don't love me for fun, girl, let me be the one, girl,
Bm7
A/C♯
1.
D
E
A
love me for a rea - son, let the rea - son be love.

2.
D/E
A/E
D
A
E
D
E
A
G9
fr4
let the rea - son be love.
D.S. al Coda
C
G/B
Gm/B♭
F/A
C/G
F
Esus4
E
Coda
A
C♯m7
D
A
Bm7
A/C♯
Don't love me for fun, girl, let me be the one, girl, love me for a rea - son,
D
E
A
C
Em7
F
C
let the rea - son be love. Don't love me for fun, girl, let me be the one, girl;

Verse 2:
Kisses and caresses are only minor tests, babe,
Of love needs and stresses between a woman and a man.
So if love everlasting isn't what you're asking,
I'll have to pass, girl; I'm proud to take a stand.
I can't continue guessing, because it's only messing
With my pride and my mind.
So write down this time to time:

To Chorus

Verse 3:
I'm just a little old-fashioned,
It takes more than a physical attraction.
My initial reaction is "Honey, give me love;
Not a facsimile of."

To Chorus

picture of you

Words & Music by Eliot Kennedy, Ronan Keating, Paul Wilson & Andy Watkins.

♩=116
C
G6/B
Gm7
fr3
F
G
C
G6/B
Gm7
fr3
F
G
C
G/B
Gm7
fr3
Did-n't I say that I would make a mis-take?__ Did-n't they say you were gon-
F
G
C
G/B
- na be trou - ble?_ Lay parts on me who were too much to take, I could-n't see

Gm7
fr3
F
G
C
it, I did-n't want to know.
I let you in and you
(Verse 2 see block lyric)
G/B
Gm7
fr3
let me down.
You messed me up and you turned
F
G
C
G/B
my life a - round. Left me feel-ing I had no-where to go, I was a - lone,
Gm7
fr3
F
how was I to know that?

Dm11
fr5
Am7
G
You were with me there when I need - ed some - bo - dy.
G13
fr3
You were with me there, the on - ly one to help me.
CHORUS
C
G6/B
Gm7
I had a pic - ture of you in my mind, nev - er knew
F
G7
it could be so wrong, Why'd it take me so long just to find

1.
Gm7
fr3
F
G7
C
the friend that was there all a - long?
G/B
Gm7
fr3
F
G
2.
C
Instrumental ad lib.
G/B
Gm7
fr3
F
G
C
G/B

Verse 2:
Do you believe that after all that we've been through
I'd be able to put my trust in you?
Goes to show you can forgive and forget
Looking back I have no regrets, cos

You were with me there *etc.*

when all is said and done

Words & Music by Martin Brannigan, Stephen Gately, Ronan Keating, Michael Graham, Shane Lynch, Keith Duffy & Ray Hedges.

♩= 80
E♭m
D♭
D♭sus4
fr4
C♭
Ped.
✽ Ped.
✽ etc. sim.
1. Days that we spent when I was so small,
(Verse 2 see block lyric)
ne-ver let me fall,
you ne-ver let me fall.

E♭m
D♭
Taught me to see the right and the wrong;
C♭
D♭
oh, I'm not that strong, wish I was that strong.
E♭m
D♭
You've been good to me, tending my ev - 'ry
C♭
E♭m
D♭
need. Just look what I am,

D♭/F
E♭/G
fr3
F/A
G/B
C
can't you see, it's you in me?
When all is said and done,
F
C
look be - fore you
C/G
G
C/E
F
I'm your son.
Can't you see it's
G
Am
G
you in me,
a man.

Verse 2:
Now I'm a man, time has gone fast;
I didn't want it to, I didn't want it to.
Went on my way like a crazy young fool;
I never wanted to, I never wanted to.
You've been good *etc.*

words

Words & Music by Barry Gibb, Robin Gibb & Maurice Gibb.

Moderately slow

mp legato

G

Smile an ev - er - last - ing smile; a smile could bring you

A

near to me.

D

Don't ev - er let me find you

C
G
gone 'cause that would bring a tear to me. This
B♭
world has lost its glo - ry; let's start a brand - new sto - ry
F
G
now, my love. Right now, there'll be no oth - er
A
D
time, and I can show you how, my love.

G
A
mf
Talk in ev - er - last - ing words and ded - i - cate them all to me.
D
And I will give you all my life, I'm here if you should
C
G
B♭
call to me.
You think that I don't e - ven
D
N.C.
mean a sin - gle word I say.
It's on - ly

G
D
words, and words are all I have to take your heart a-
G
D
N.C.
G
way. It's on-ly words, and words are all I
D
G
D
N.C.
have to take your heart a-way. It's on-ly
G
words, and words are all I have to take your heart a-way.
rit.
mp

so good

Words & Music by Martin Brannigan, Stephen Gately, Ronan Keating, Michael Graham, Shane Lynch, Keith Duffy & Ray Hedges.

D
A
E
Dmaj7
like I knew we should.
G/A
A
fr3
1. I've heard it be - fore, oh yeah, and you're tell - ing me no,
See Block Lyrics for Verse 2
and I'm cra - zy. We're talk - ing too fast, we've just got - ta
take it nice and slow, sit back let it flow now.

E
D
E
Don't be mis-un-der-stood, when ba-by, may-be you know:
D
A
D
A
D
A
We're gon-na be so good, like I knew we would, like on-ly we could,
E
Dmaj7
A
D
A
come on and hear me now. Gon-na be so good 'cos it's un-der-stood,
To Coda
D
A
E
Dmaj7
like I knew we should, oh, oh, so good now ba-by.

1.
G/A
A7
G/A
A7
We're gon - na be so good,
N.C.
don't you know that we could be good.
2.
A
E/A
A
E/A
A
E/A
A
E/A
A
E/A
Be so good,
A
E/A
A
E/A
N.C.
D.%. al Coda
be so good now, be so good.

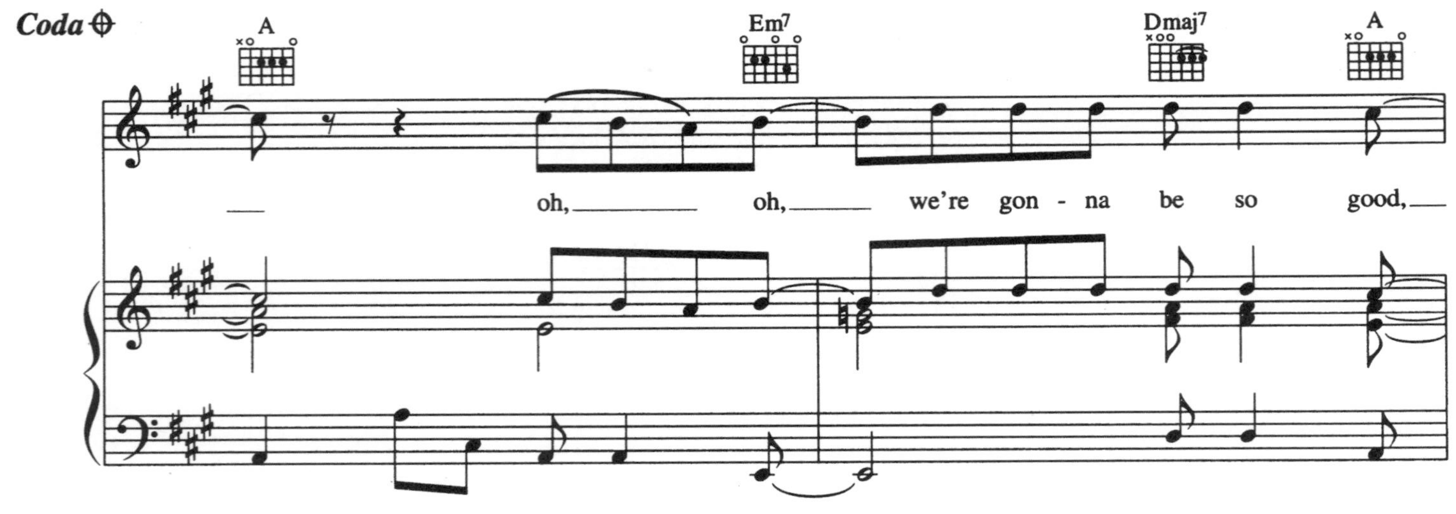

Verse 2:
No matter the cost
When we're out on the town getting lazy
I'll show you who's boss
We're just gonna take it all the way
No matter what they say now.